How to Be the GREATEST WRITER in the WORLD

Written by Matt Cibula
Illustrated by Brian Strassburg

Zino Press
CHILDREN'S BOOKS

Madison, Wisconsin

How to Be the Greatest Writer in the World is published by
Zino Press Children's Books, PO Box 52, Madison, Wisconsin 53701. Text
copyright © 1999 by Matt Cibula. Illustrations copyright © 1999 by Zino Press
Children's Books. Entire contents copyright © 1999 by Zino Press Children's
Books. All rights reserved. No parts of this book may be reproduced in any way,
except for brief excerpts for purposes of review in newspapers and magazines,
without the expressed written permission of Zino Press Children's Books. Printed
in U.S.A.

Edited by Dave Schreiner. Designed by Ann Kniskern.

Cibula, Matt S.
     How to Be the greatest writer in the world / written by Matt Cibula ;
illustrated by Brian Strassburg.
          p.   cm.
     Summary: Presents eighty-eight imaginative writing exercises designed
to spark creativity, focusing on vocabulary, brainstorming, description,
fiction, non-fiction, and poetry.
     ISBN 1-55933-276-X
     1. English language Composition and exercises Juvenile literature.
(1. English language — Composition and exercises. 2. Creative writing.)
I. Strassburg, Brian, ill. II. Title.
LB1576.C5568 1999
808' .042—DC21
                                                              99-27178
                                                              CIP

10 9 8 7 6 5 4 3 2 1

Introduction

I usually skip introductions because they're boring, so I won't be offended if you do the same and get straight to the real part of the book. However, I thought I should explain eleven things right here at the beginning.

1. This book contains 88 writing exercises, all of which should help you in your quest to be The Greatest Writer in the World.

2. It also features illustrations by Brian Strassburg, who is a good friend, a professional cartoonist, and a surprisingly good basketball player.

3. I've been a writer since second grade, which is how I came up with most of these exercises. This book is meant to help you avoid the biggest problem I had as a young writer: "I don't know what to write about."

4. The exercises are listed the way they are because I think it's the best order. You can do the exercises in order, or not.

5. I'm not saying I am The Greatest Writer in the World. But when I do something great, when I write a poem or play or story or children's book or letter or report and it's perfect — then I feel like The Greatest Writer in the World. And when you do one of these exercises perfectly you'll feel like The Greatest Writer in the World too. That's what we're after here.

6. Find the way you write best and stick with it. I personally have to be listening to softly-playing jazz. I use an ink pen filled with either black or blue ink and I write in a big college-ruled notebook — but that's just me. If you can crank loud music while sitting at a computer drinking soda and still write great stuff, good for you.

7. Don't lose your good writing. Use a single notebook or file everything in the same folder or binder. If you write on a computer, put all your work in one big folder. Learn from my mistakes; I'm still looking for a hilarious song I once wrote. I *know* it's here somewhere.

8. Don't just whip through this book. Relax. Take your time. If you want to do an exercise three or seven times, do it.

9. Don't be afraid to be ridiculous. It's worked for me.

10. Don't be afraid to be serious, either.

11. Big, huge, Brobdignagian shout-outs to the Zino editorial and graphics staff, my family, and all the schools who've let me come in and be weird.

1 Starting is the hardest part.

Nothing is worse than seeing that blank page in front of you. I hate that feeling. That's why I came up with this book, and that's why we're starting with this exercise. This might be a good one to come back to if you ever run out of ideas.

Exercise . . . .

Write the end of a story. Any story at all. If you can't think of one, you can use "And they lived happily ever after." Once you write that, work backwards: Who are "they"? What were they doing right before the story ended? And then before that? Keep going until you get to the start. It's sneaky, but it works.

2 Sprint through your day.

It's best to keep a separate notebook as a journal. Journals are really important for writers, but they're hard to do. (You don't always have time to write every single night, you might be tired or cranky, etc.) This is the best way I've found to keep a journal; it helps get down the basic facts, and you can write more if you have time. But if you don't do it every night it won't work. So do it, and no excuses.

Exercise . . . .

For every day, make the following lists:

❶ The five best things that happened today.
❷ The three worst things that happened today.
❸ The most surprising thing that happened today.
❹ The most important thing I learned today.

Whatever you want to write about each of these items is up to you.

3 Back in the days...

You have to keep checking in with yourself as a writer and remember who you used to be. Otherwise your characters won't be real, because they won't be able to change over time. It's also just kind of fun to think about yourself as a younger person, especially now that you're older and more mature.

Exercise . . . .

What were you doing exactly one year ago? What did you look like? Whose class were you in? Who were your friends? Your enemies? What was your favorite song and movie and book back then? Now, how about two years ago? Three? Five? Ten?

4 The ABC style.

I first made this game up when I was in sixth grade. I spent an entire summer doing this. I wasn't exactly the coolest kid, as you might imagine, but when I was able to do one of these right, I *felt* pretty cool.

Exercise . . . .

Write a paragraph where the first word starts with the letter A, the second word with B, and so on until you get to Z. If you can do this, try starting with Z and going backwards. And if you can do that, try this one: pick a letter and then write a sentence where every word begins with that letter.

5 Read really good books.

Look — writers read, and that's that. If you don't read good books, how will you know what one is? Read everywhere. Read anytime you can. Read for fun. Read in the car on long or short trips (unless you get sick, in which case, don't).

Exercise . . . .

Think about all the books you've read in your life, then make a list of your 50 favorites. You don't have to rank them in order unless you want to. Trade your list with a friend. How many books do you two have in common? Try to read all the books on your friend's list, too!

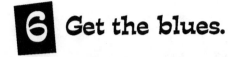

6 Get the blues.

"She walked into the room wearing a blue shirt."

Okay, nice start, but not very helpful. "Blue"? There must
be hundreds of kinds of blue. There are people whose job it is
to come up with names for colors of blue. If you want people
to notice the things you say, don't be lazy and just say "blue"
when you see that shirt in your mind as "turquoise" or "navy" or
"sapphire."

Exercise . . . .

List every blue you've ever heard of in your life.
Crayon colors, shades of blue you see in clothes
catalogues or in the paint sections of hardware
stores, blues of sports teams and eye shadow
names — all are fair. When you get to 300, you've
done enough on this exercise, and it's time to
stop, because you're getting a little obsessed.

7 Invent the blues.

But just listing all the blues other people have ever invented is
only the first part of the game. You have to go beyond that.
How? By making stuff up. Don't you think your readers will sit up
and take notice if your characters walk into a room wearing a
shirt the color of old dried toothpaste? Or if someone is driving
a car as blue as Superman's hair?

Exercise . . . .

Make up blues you've never heard of before, or
that no one's ever thought of before. I know you
can think of at least 103 of these.

Extra credit

Do this with
another color.

8 Get inside your TV.

Admit it: you watch television. I don't think TV is bad; it's fun and sometimes interesting, and unless you watch it too much it won't kill your creativity. But writers watch differently than other people; we watch to practice our skills!

Exercise . . . .

Write an episode of your favorite TV show. Include the major characters and any other characters you want to, and have them say and do the kinds of things they say and do on the show. Don't be afraid that you're not a TV writer; they weren't born writing TV shows any more than you were. They just practiced a lot. So start practicing.

9 Learn your geography.

Sorry that the title sounds so much like "Eat your vegetables." Hey, you have to learn about the world and the things in it. You will have a very hard time writing a story that takes place in Cairo, Egypt, if you know nothing about it or where it is.

Exercise . . . .

Challenge yourself to learn about one new foreign country a week for a year. Do some research! Where is that country? How big is it? What languages do they speak there? What is interesting about it? Please don't take the easy way out and go by stereotypes. That's what bad writers do.

10 Create a whole new world.

Now that you're learning about the countries that are actually out there, it's time to make one up. Why? Because once you invent a place, you can set your stories there and no one can tell you you're wrong about any details, that's why.

Exercise . . . .

Draw a shape on a piece of paper. That's your new country (or county or city or state or province or island or whatever you want). Then fill in the details. Where's the capital city? The other cities and towns? What are they called? Where are the rivers, the oceans, the lakes? Where are the farms and the forests? What other lands share a border with your new nation? What does your flag look like?

 11 Outer space.

I think all writers are at least a little bit fascinated by space and other planets. Who wouldn't get excited about dreaming up a whole new way to live?

Exercise . . . .

Pick a planet from our solar system. Learn about it and then write about what it would be like to live there. You can be a human astronaut or a made-up alien species. Describe your house, if you have one; your school and family and pets, if you have them; your daily routine.

Extra credit

Make up an entirely new planet and describe it thoroughly.

12 Notice people.

Creating convincing human characters is one of the most difficult things you can do as a writer. You have to start practicing right away. The first step is to cheat by observing actual living people. One of my favorite writers, Eudora Welty, once said writers cannot be afraid to stare at people they don't know. Just don't do this on the New York subway. I've tried.

Exercise . . . .

Physically describe someone you know. The best way to do this is to get that person's permission and then just stare at her or him for a while, taking notes. Then turn your notes into a page or two or three describing that person *without* saying anything about personality. If you stare at someone without his or her permission, prepare to get smacked. Then again, if you don't care. . .

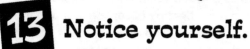 13 Notice yourself.

Writers spend a lot of time staring into mirrors. Are we just that
good looking? Maybe. But I think we want to look at ourselves
to get to know ourselves better, considering we spend so much
time thinking about other characters and their struggles. . . or
maybe it's just because we *are* that good looking.

Exercise . . . .

Describe yourself as fairly as you can. Don't use a
lot of "good" or "bad" words, and don't talk
about your feelings or your likes and dislikes. Just
write what you see in the mirror.

14 Get others to notice you.

There is always a difference between the way people see themselves and the way others see them. This also applies to writers and artists. The sooner you learn this lesson, the better for you as a writer.

Exercise . . . .

Now let someone else describe you in writing. (Again, this should just be a *physical* description.) When that person is done, read what he or she wrote. How different is it from what you wrote in **Exercise 13**?

Extra credit

Return the favor and describe your friend.

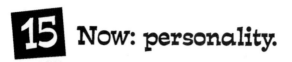
Physical description is very different from describing what someone is really like. For example, the biggest strongest kid in my sixth grade class was also the gentlest and nicest person I've ever known. Just look at everyone as a real person — someone different from all other people — and you'll probably be okay.

Exercise . . . .

Pick someone you know very well and describe exactly who that person is. Use examples; it doesn't help to just say someone is very cool if you don't show their cool-ness in action. If you add some physical details at this point, that's all right, but you don't have to. This exercise is all about inner qualities.

16 Now: you.

Being honest with yourself about yourself is one of the toughest things you will ever have to do in your life. It will take your entire time on this planet to learn this skill, and you will sometimes not be happy with what you observe. But most of the time you will end up saying, "You know? I'm not so bad."

Exercise . . . .

Write five paragraphs — or more — telling exactly who you are on the *inside*. Again, examples are good and details are important. It might be easier just to make a list of things you know about your- self (likes, dislikes, skills, dreams, etc.) and then put that in paragraph form.

17 Make the leap.

Now that you've practiced with real people, including yourself, you're ready for fake people, or characters. These are people you make up, so you're responsible for them. Don't sell them out — work hard on them! Be proud of them, they're yours. And feel free to like or dislike anyone you invent.

Exercise . . . .

Do brief profiles of ten made-up characters. Tell everything about them, from what they look like to how they think and act — but *don't* give them names yet. If you can't stop when you get to ten, then you are becoming a writer.

18 Names.

It is very hard for me to come up with good names for my characters. Matching a name to a personality is hard. That's what makes it fun. If you spend a lot of time on a character and then give her or him a fakey name, readers will be confused.

Exercise . . . .

Name the characters you just invented in **Exercise 17**. Try to give them real names, names actual people could have. That doesn't mean make them boring, run-of-the-mill names. Now hide these names and let someone else make up names for your characters. Do the same for that person's characters. Any surprises?

19 All about the music.

When you watch a movie, pay careful attention to the sound-track music. It's almost like a separate character, because it can set whatever mood the director wants: sad, happy, scary, or anything else.

Exercise . . . .

Put on any music you want and *really listen* to it. Then describe the scene in a made-up movie that would have that music as background. See the scene in your head and write it down.

Extra credit
Now write the next two scenes.

Thelonious Monk.

This looks like a made-up name, but it's not; Monk was a great jazz pianist and songwriter who just happened to have an incredibly amazing name. (His middle name was Sphere.) Other real names on my list of The Best Names Ever: Learned Hand and Kenesaw Mountain Landis, who were judges; Myrna Loy (actress); Vaughn Buffalo (guy I went to college with); and Amos Tutuola (awesome Nigerian writer).

Exercise . . . .

Compile your own list of The Best Names Ever. They all have to be the names of real people, but they don't all have to be like Judge Learned Hand. Just a name that sounds or looks good to you will do.

21 It's not where you're from, it's where you live.

I never have been really big on writers who spend a lot of time describing rooms and houses, unless it was very important to the plot of the book. Very often, I think, writers do things because they think they're supposed to, not because they need to. But now that I've said all that, I will say that sometimes it's very important for a reader to know exactly what a room looks like.

Exercise . . . .

Write about where you live, from the inside out. Start with your room, and use details: colors, furniture, size of the room, how the room makes you feel, etc. Then narrate a tour of your apartment or house, room by room.

22 This one will take a while.

In order to write well, you have to observe well. This does not just mean looking; it means smelling, touching, tasting, hearing, and feeling too. It also means you have to be able to write down what you observe. (This will help teach patience, too, because you won't be done for a year.)

Exercise ....

Step 1: Choose some place outside to observe, and then observe the heck out of it. List every observation you have about that place, and then write three paragraphs or more about it.

Step 2: Wait exactly three months and do it again. What has changed?

Step 3: Repeat three months later.

Step 4: Do the whole thing again one final time three months after that. Now compare your four observations. What has changed most? What hasn't changed at all?

This isn't writing.

In order to be a great writer, you sometimes have to stop writing. You have to read, you have to experience life and do chores and homework and sleep and everything else that isn't writing. Learning new skills is very valuable for your authorial development, especially if they are skills you never thought you'd be able to learn. That's why I picked drawing.

Exercise . . . .

Draw something until it looks real. It doesn't matter if you pick a street corner or a stuffed monkey — just start sketching. (I chose the monkey, because it doesn't move.) When you finish, look at what you've done — pretty good but it could be better, right? Try again. Be tough with yourself on this one: have you really captured what you were trying to capture? No? Try again.

24 Pure silliness.

The other day my daughter, Emma, who is three and a half years old, said I was standing on the blund. When I asked what a blund was, she said, "It's sort of like the floor and a rug." I don't think anyone has ever called a floor with a rug on it a blund before. My daughter is a genius.

Exercise . . . .

Make up words. Figure out what they mean, or not. Maybe they make a little bit of sense ("salibration" is celebrating so hard you salivate. This word was made up by William Beans after the Crossroads Junior High School basketball team won its first game) or maybe they make no sense at all, like "blund." Compile a list of words you invented. Cherish that list.

25 Temperature.

Some writers make it rain when a character is sad, make the sun come out when she or he is happy, whip up a storm when the character is troubled, etc. This is called the "pathetic fallacy." I guess this isn't the worst thing to do in a story, but it's just too easy. So don't do it.

Exercise . . . .

Write two pieces from your memory. The first one should be entitled, "The Coldest Day of My Life," and should tell what was happening on the physically coldest day you remember. (We're only talking weather here.) The second one? You guessed it: "The Hottest Day of My Life." Think: did the weather have anything to do with your mood? Did your mood make the weather seem different?

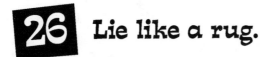

26 Lie like a rug.

Telling the truth is very important. I personally have never gotten away with a lie, so I don't lie in real life. But writing isn't real life. Luckily for the world, many writers choose to stretch, bend, and otherwise mess with the facts of the world. I am among them, and I am going to encourage you to do the same. If this makes you uncomfortable, then just think of this: sometimes you can teach more people about the truth by making up a good story.

Exercise . . . .

Make up a big lie about why you don't have your homework. Remember, it's the little details that make people believe the story. And since you're not actually going to tell this tall tale to your teacher — because you always finish your homework, right? — the stranger and more unlikely your lie is, the better. Now compare your lie with your friends'. Whose is best?

27 Groceries, part 1.

Most of us take food for granted. It's always there at the store, never runs out, tastes good, all that stuff. But do we really appreciate what we have? I doubt it. Food columnists, restaurant critics, and cookbook writers all have excellent jobs. Imagine getting paid to write about eating! Well, they're not the only ones who can talk about food.

Exercise . . . .

Make a list of every meal you eat in one week. (Don't include tiny snacks.) Then write down four things:

❶ Where and with whom did you eat each of your meals?
❷ What was the best thing you ate all week? (Describe it lovingly.)
❸ What was the worst thing you ate all week? (Make sure it seems nasty to us as well.)
❹ What is the greatest meal you ever had? Why? (Be specific!)

28 Salute your elders.

My fifth grade teacher Miss Johnson was probably the one who was most important to me as a writer, because she really understood me and encouraged me. Then again, maybe it was Mrs. Murphy in second grade, when she let me direct my first play ("A Treehouse in New England") for the class. Or Mr. Gettel in sixth grade when he taught me not to worry about what other people think. And I can't forget Ms. Birnbaum and Mr. Nichols in high school, or Ms. Kroese in junior high. Wow — it's hard to leave anyone out. But this isn't about me, now, is it?

Exercise . . . .

Write about the best teacher you have ever had. What makes this teacher so important to you? What did you learn from him or her? If you want to, you can write a letter to your teacher and express your feelings directly.

29 How does that thing work?

Most people think creative writing has to be fiction, plays, and poetry. But writing about true things can be just as creative as any other writing you do. You have to make the world come alive to the reader, no matter what you write.

Exercise . . . .

Tell me how a car engine works. If you don't know, you can look it up or ask a friend or teacher or parent. It's important that you write this information down and make it interesting. If you don't do that the first time, try again and jazz it up a little.

30 Blow it up.

A good word to know is hyperbole (pronounced hy-PUR-buh-lee). This is basically the same word as exaggeration (ex-ajj-ur-AY-shun); both mean that someone is making something seem much bigger or more important than it really is. Here's an example: instead of writing, "He is really tall," you might use hyperbole — "He's as big as the Empire State Building." An extreme example of this: "He's so big, he calls Godzilla 'Shorty.'" A different example: "He's so small, he was an extra in *A Bug's Life*."

Exercise ....

Start practicing this important skill, or rather start writing down good examples, since you're probably doing this all the time anyway. Try not to use ones you've used before, because the aim of good hyperbole is to make the reader understand something in a brand-new way, and the best way to do that is to use the freshest phrases.

31 Not quite as weird as a frog in a tutu.

Litotes (ly-TOAT-iz) is kind of the weird cousin of hyperbole; it's a sort of backwards way of exaggerating. Instead of saying that something is really big or small or weird, you say that isn't *quite* the case. Examples: "She's not quite as tall as Shaquille O'Neal," or "Him? Stuck up? Oh, no; he only kisses the mirror once a day." This might seem hard to learn, but it's certainly easier than doing algebra at the bottom of a mineshaft at midnight.

Exercise . . . .

Try a few! Here are some ideas to get you started. For a really smart girl: "She's not so smart...."For something dangerous: "That's almost as safe as...." If you can come up with some good ones, e-mail them to me at the address in the back of the book, and please put "litotes" in the Subject line so I know that it's you.

32 It looks like "smile."

When you compare two things that aren't really alike except in one important way and you use the words "like," "than," or "as," you're inventing a simile (pronounced SIM-ih-lee). For example, if you were using a simile to describe a red-haired kid you might say, "His hair was like a fire on his head." You hear a lot of similes in rap and popular music because they're direct and simple to do.

Exercise . . . .

Invent 57 similes. Try one a day for 57 days. It's as fun as a day at Disneyland, easier than falling off a bouncing basketball, and useful like pockets. Okay, you can have those three free of charge. Now you only have to do 54 similes. Don't say I never did anything for you.

33 What's a meta for?

A metaphor (MET-a-for) is just like a simile, except that you don't use "as" or "than" or "like" in between the things you're comparing. Instead of the simile "That guy is as cool as ice cream," you could just say "That guy is ice cream." A fast bird zooming between trees becomes an arrow, and a loud car can be a storm on wheels or a stampede of rhinos coming down the street.

Exercise . . . .

I will only make you write 39 metaphors. You can write more if you want, but that's only if you want to be really truly great. Please don't try to write all 39 in one sitting.

34 This won't make much sense to chimpanzees.

Here's another word I'm going to throw at you: personification (say it like per-sahn-ih-fih-KAY-shun), which is when you give human thoughts and feelings to things that aren't human. (Person-ification — get it?) For example, if you say, "The house looks out over the happy street," you're doing a double personification because 1) the house is looking, and 2) the street is happy.

Exercise . . . .

Find a pair of shoes and study them. Then make up a personification for them: are they tired? Perky? Stuck-up? Then choose sixteen other non-human objects and do the same for them.

35 The best word ever.

Here is a word you should add to your list of truly great words: onomatopoeia (ahn-o-mah-toh-PEE-ya). This is a Greek word that describes words that come from sounds. "Splat" is only a word because when you throw, say, a wet washrag on the floor, it goes "splat." That's onomatopoeia. Some people think onomatopoeia may be how humans started speaking in the first place, so scream or splutter or yell or whisper or mutter "onomatopoeia" every chance you get.

Exercise . . . .

Make a list of all the onomatopoeic words you can. This will end up being a very long list if you pay attention, so reserve a couple of pages in your notebook for it. Also, learn to spell and correctly pronounce onomatopoeia. It's the kind of word that will freak out your parents and teachers and make them realize you are the brilliant genius that you are.

36 Collect these so you can stay away from them.

What we're talking about here are clichés (klih-SHAYS), and they are considered very very bad. What are they? They're phrases that have been used so often that they've lost all their impact. For example, if you call someone "cute as a button," that's a cliché, because that has been used about one hundred bazillion times in the history of the world. (Also: what's so cute about a button?) "Happy as a lark" is a cliché; "easy as pie" is a cliché. And what's the point of saying things that have already been said so often?

Exercise . . . .

The first step here is to list any other overused clichés you know. (Hint: if adults are using a phrase that only kids used to use, it has probably become a cliché.) The second step is to survey your friends, teachers, and family members to get their opinions about what words, phrases, sayings, and figures of speech they think are clichéd. Step three is to avoid all of them.

 **37** Groceries, part 2.

One of the hardest — and simplest — things to do is to cook well. You need to be able to read instructions and follow them, but if you do it right you can eat something you made all by yourself. Then you can start getting funky with new ingredients and making up brand-new meals you've never had before. Sounds a lot like writing, doesn't it?

Exercise . . . .

Start with something really easy that you know how to make, like a sandwich or a bowl of cereal. Write a story about fixing that meal in which you talk about every single detail of the process. Then pick something harder, like pasta. Watch carefully as your mom or your Uncle Fenwick or whoever makes it, and again describe every single detail. (This is also helpful because almost all writers are poor for a while and have to do things like make their own pasta.)

38 Be that famous person.

If you keep trying, you could be rich and famous and successful someday. The only way you'll be ready for your future celebrity status is to practice now. After all, your big break could be tomorrow. You had better be prepared.

Exercise . . . .

Practice being famous. When you are interviewed, you have to be ready to talk about yourself. How would you describe your newest book? Why did you decide to write about this subject? What are you proudest of about this book? What's your next book going to be about? What's the best thing about being famous and rich? What does your house look like? Answer these questions and anything else your interviewer asks you. Oh, and you'd better work on that autograph.

39 Real news.

You have to know how to write a news story, so here goes. First of all, don't write what you think or what you feel; just tell the facts as you know them. The second thing to remember is that news stories have to give the answers to the "five W" questions: Who? What? When? Where? and Why? These questions should be answered first in a news story, in short sentences. "Author Matt Cibula had a huge salad for dinner yesterday at his home in Madison, Wisconsin. When asked why, he replied, 'Because I had already eaten all the veggie dogs and there was no pasta left.'" Then go on to tell the rest of the story.

Exercise . . . .

Pick something that happened yesterday and write a news story about it. Make the reader care deeply about it. If you need to interview people, do so.

40 Avoid saying "said."

You don't always have to indicate that someone talked by saying "he said" or "she said." There are so many other more graceful and descriptive words and terms to show that someone spoke, or whispered, or shrieked. Good writers know about the words. Great writers actually use them.

Exercise . . . .

Make a list of 51 words for "said." Keep this list in your notebook, and use it. It's a working list, and it should keep growing over your whole writing career.

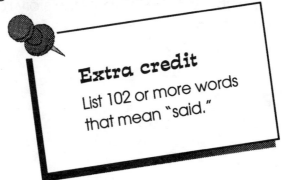

Extra credit
List 102 or more words that mean "said."

41 Ready, willing, and fable.

Fables are short stories that teach lessons or morals, usually using animal characters that talk and act like humans. The best way to write a fable is to work backwards: choose the moral or lesson of the story first, then think about how you're going to convince someone that the moral is important and true. Pick your animals carefully; they all should have distinct personalities and character traits.

Exercise . . . .

Read at least ten fables, and don't just read ten Aesops in a row. (I recommend some Anansi the Spider stories from Africa; there are many others.) Now write four fables yourself. Make sure you end each one with "And the moral of the story is..." followed by the moral of your story.

42 Sporty.

I played a lot of sports as a kid, and I enjoyed most of them. Mostly what I liked was being around other kids, learning the rules, and then trying to be really good at whatever I did. I always tried to work very hard in practice, and it taught me how to work hard to get things done.

Exercise . . . .

What is your favorite sport? Write a piece about it. This can be in paragraph form or a poem or a play or a movie scene or a list or anything you want. Tell what you like about it, maybe write about some of your favorite players, it's up to you. Write as if you are trying to explain the sport to someone who doesn't like it as much as you do.

43 Qcapcr ambcq.
(Secret codes.)

In the title of this exercise, I rewrote the phrase "secret codes" by taking each letter and replacing it with the letter two letters before it in the alphabet (s = q, e = c, and on like that). That's not a very sneaky code, but it would be pretty hard to figure out if you didn't know the secret. Pgefr?

Exercise . . . .

Make up a language of your own. It can be a substitution code, like the one I just showed you, or it can be a completely weird one from your own imagination. Make sure you know all the rules to your language, and write them all down. Now try to write a story using your new language. Or share the rules with a (trusted) friend and write notes to each other — but not in class, or your teacher will catch you and read them out loud and you'll be embarrassed.

44 100 is a good number.

I thought I invented this kind of poem, and I was very proud of myself until I heard that my friend Joel was already writing the exact same kind of poem. Is it coincidence? Or fate?

Exercise . . . .

Write a poem of exactly 100 words — no more, no less. Yes, words with a hyphen in them count as only one word. No, the title does not count. No, it doesn't even have to be a poem. Try to write a newspaper article, a speech, a story of 100 words.

Extra credit
Write a play in which the characters speak a total of exactly 100 words.

45 Let your characters strut.

Everything I said before about the word "said" goes double for "walked." Everyone uses the word "walked" too much; depending on my mood, I'll stroll or strut or stride or stagger, or any number of things. Now my editor is worried that no one will ever use the word "walk" again, so just try to work these new ways to "walk" into your other writing when it makes sense.

Exercise . . . .

Make a list of 75 different ways of expressing that a character is taking steps with her or his feet.

Extra credit
One hundred fifty ways.
(But don't take stroll or strut or stride or stagger. They're mine!)

 46 Time machine.

I like my life right now just fine. But I would love to be able to go back to New York in 1958 and see and meet all the great jazz musicians whose work I love, or to America or Africa before the Europeans came to see what it was really like, or to England in 1598 to see a Shakespeare play live at the Globe Theater. If I only knew how to build one of those time machines.

Exercise . . . .

If you could travel to any other time and place in history, what would it be? Why? Write a story where you get to do just that. What is it like? Don't forget that you will probably have some problems fitting in. . .

47 Fix it.

We've all read a book or story or something that just didn't end the way we wanted it to. I can think of at least eleven books that I loved until the last three chapters. Don't you hate that?

Exercise . . . .

Find a book or story or poem that needs a new ending, and write it. Keep to the same style as the original writer, and don't make it too weird, but just write the end of the story that you think should be there instead of the old one.

Extra credit
Do the same thing for a book with an ending you do like.

48 Ranking the presidents.

Sooner or later, you'll have to learn a lot of facts about all the presidents the United States has had. This could be boring, but it doesn't have to be. There is something interesting to learn that you never knew before about every president, even if no one ever talks about that one any more.

Exercise . . . .

List your three favorite U.S. presidents. Do some research on them. Explain why they are your favorites and include lots of information about them. If it helps, pick one of them and write a story based on that president dealing with an important problem he faced.

49 Know the history of your words.

Whenever I got in trouble in Mr. Gettel's class, he made me copy pages out of the big huge unabridged dictionary in our classroom. I really didn't mind, though, because huge dictionaries tell you lots of stuff. For instance, they tell you what language every word comes from. You can find out how words were spelled hundreds of years ago, or what they used to mean back when they were invented.

Exercise ....

Pick ten words from any of the word lists you've made for any of the exercises in this book. Then find out where these words came from, what they used to mean, and what they mean today. This is probably a library assignment, unless you have one of those big old dictionaries lying around; ask your friendly librarian for help.

50 Easiest one in the book.

My favorite poetic form comes from "troubadour" poetry. The *enueg* (EN-yoo-egg; it means "annoyance") is a style in which the poet lists everything that annoys him or her that day: big things, small things, anything at all.

Exercise . . . .

Write an *enueg* every Wednesday for a month. Compare them: what annoys you most often? (This is a good one to return to if you're too annoyed to write anything else.)

51 Speech.

Dialogue originally meant two people talking, but it can also mean anytime a character speaks in novels, stories, or other writing. Dialogue is the most fun for me to write, but I think writing good dialogue is very difficult. Everyone thinks they are able to write down the way people talk, but some writers don't spend enough time listening to how people really sound when they talk. But not us!

Exercise . . . .

Go somewhere that you can hear other people talking. Listen and write down exactly what you hear, even if it's the product of two or three different conversations. One warning: if you hear people discussing where they hid the body, you picked the wrong conversation to overhear. Walk away slowly.

52 Say it loud.

The easiest way to write dialogue is just to put conversations
down on paper and leave it to the reader to hear those voices
in his or her head. Unfortunately, that is also the worst way. If
your dialogue is going to have snap and style and actually
sound like people talking, you have to actually hear it out loud.
Say it yourself, or have your friends speak it for you, or anything
you have to do, but you have to hear it yourself.

Exercise . . . .

Write a story with nothing in it except two people
talking. (Yes, you can cheat a little, but not too
much.) Maybe they're talking on the telephone,
or in a crowded restaurant; maybe they're friends,
or enemies, or strangers. Concentrate on making
their words sound like words that these two people
would actually say to each other. Now recite it out
loud. Does it sound natural?

53 Take a hike.

I went for a stroll today. I saw some beautiful ducks trying to stay out of the way of an angry-looking swan. I noticed that I walked just about as fast as the tempo of the Miles Davis song "E.S.P.," which was playing in my head. I overheard a hilarious conversation between two guys in a store. It was a great day.

Exercise . . . .

Find your good walking shoes and go. Use all your senses and really be attentive to what's going on all around you. Try to notice things you never noticed before, or things you've known for a while but forgot. And when you get back home, write it down. If this is hard at first, try again — you'll get the hang of it. Then you'll want to do it all the time.

54 Pass it around.

Because I prefer books, I am not as interested in the Internet as some people are, but I think e-mail is pretty amazing. It helps me keep in touch with people in a way that would be a lot tougher — and more expensive — to do on the phone. E-mail is perfectly adapted for this exercise, which we used to do back when we didn't have computers...or automobiles...or electric light...

Exercise . . . .

Start a story. E-mail what you write to a friend. Now let him or her write the next part and e-mail it back to you. (If you don't have e-mail, paper will suffice.) Keep that up for a while; you'll know when to end it. Make sure you and your friend are both writing the same story, because it won't work if you don't cooperate. This is even more fun with more people involved.

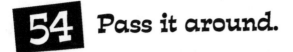

55 Groceries, part 3.

Chefs cook meals the way writers write stories. They use ingredients, we use words, but we both take them and mess with them and mix them up and see how they work together. I never liked to cook until I figured this out, but now I love to cook. And just as writers need to know a lot about words, cooks need to learn a lot about ingredients.

Exercise . . . .

List 26 vegetables and 26 fruits. How many of them have you eaten? How many have you ever seen? Which do you love? Which do you hate? Why?

Extra credit
List them in size order:
biggest to smallest.

56 Fake news.

Sure, anyone can look at a picture in the newspaper, read the caption, and figure out what happened. It takes a real writer to skip reading the caption.

Exercise . . . .

Cut a picture out of the paper, with the caption not attached. Find a friend who will do the same, and then trade pictures. Now write a good caption for the picture your friend gave you. Include all the made-up details you can. Now write an article to go along with your caption and the picture. How close were you to the real news story? How close was your friend?

57 In dreams begins great writing.

Everyone has had the horrible experience of having a really fantastic and odd dream, waking up, and then forgetting what the dream was. This is a tragedy, because dreaming is the writer's best friend. If you practice this exercise now, you will probably keep it up your entire life.

Exercise . . . .

Get a new notebook and keep it next to your bed as a Dream Journal. Every morning, write down any dreams you remember from the night before. If a dream wakes you up in the middle of the night, try to write it down quickly before you go back to sleep. Read this journal for ideas!

58 It's not really a tree.

I think everyone is convinced that his or her family is the weirdest family in the history of the world. Everyone's family does have interesting, strange, nice, heartwarming, bizarre, and memorable stories just waiting for someone to tell them. Did I tell you the one about my blind uncle getting in trouble for driving a car the wrong way on a one-way street? (I know you won't believe me, but it's true. My dad was there.)

Exercise . . . .

Do some research and capture some family stories. Ask parents, grand- and great-grandparents, aunts and uncles and cousins, anyone you can think of who can tell you tales about the people on your family tree. You'll be glad you did.

 ## 59 Learn math.

Three reasons math is important: 1) You have to be able to count your money when you're rich and famous. 2) If you fail math, you'll have to take extra math classes and that will take away from your writing time. 3) Math has lots of story problems, which are just stories.

Exercise . . . .

Invent a couple of story problems. Make them easy at first (and make sure you figure out the answers to the questions) but give the people in them real personalities, and provide some drama. For example, if James has three apples and he loses two, the important question is not "How many does he have left?" but — "Won't his mom be upset? Does this happen to James all the time? What happens to Shaina when she finds the apples? What color are they?"

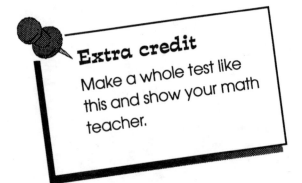

Extra credit

Make a whole test like this and show your math teacher.

60 Make it new.

My son, who is six months old as I write this, thinks everything is really exciting and fun. When he sees one of his toys he giggles and kicks his feet and smiles, even though he just saw it a few minutes ago. Babies are never bored by the world, because they are looking at it with new eyes. So what happened to us?

Exercise . . . .

Write about an ordinary object or activity, and make it seem strange, as if you had neither seen it nor heard of it before. (Maybe you're a time traveler from the past, or you come from another planet.) Describe it fully and don't cheat. How many ways can you write about a dishwasher without using the words "dish," "wash," or "machine"?

61 The senses everyone forgets.

It's very easy to write about what you see. It's fairly easy to write about what you hear and what you taste. But only great writers ever remember that they can also write about smelling things and feeling things. Personal favorite smells: bark dust, licorice, the Pad Thai at Bangkok Cuisine on Massachusetts Avenue in Boston. The best things I've ever felt? The hair on my children's heads, cold spaghetti, stepping on home plate after a home run.

Exercise . . . .

Two lists: smelling and feeling. Keep them going. You know what to do.

62 Science is your friend.

We're all scientists, it's just that some of us practice more than others. We all know that it gets dark at night because our planet spins around every day and our half has to be away from the sun for a few hours, but real scientists know all the details about it. However, it's a writer's job to explain it.

Exercise . . . .

Step 1: Pick a scientific mystery or question you've always wondered about.

Step 2: Find out how to get the information you need to solve the mystery.

Step 3: Solve the mystery.

Step 4: Write a report, starting with the problem, how you went about solving the problem, and the answer. Don't be afraid to draw pictures or diagrams if they help.

63 Tell 'em what you think.

Every writer has to have writing heroes. When you finish reading a novel or poem or newspaper article you just absolutely love, don't you want to tell the writer how you feel? Wouldn't it be great to write a message in the sky 50 miles high telling how awesome that writer is? Well, why not?

Exercise . . . .

Write a letter to the writer of your favorite book. Tell him or her what you liked about it, and talk about your own writing ambitions. You can even send your letter to the publishing company; you'll usually find the address on one of the first pages of the book. Take it from me: authors love hearing from people who read their books.

64 Harold Phlangahan.

When I was very young I had three main imaginary friends who spoke to me: my two blankets (Little Blanky and Pittle Panky) and Stephen, who operated the elevator that took food from my mouth down to my stomach. My brother Tim didn't have anyone like that when he was little, so when he was 15 he invented Harold Phlangahan, who was a bouncer and a disc jockey. His quote: "It's never too late to have a 7'4" imaginary friend."

Exercise . . . .

Write about any imaginary friends you had as a child or anything that was especially important for your imagination, whether it was a doll or a toy or a talking shoe. What did you call it? What did you talk about? What adventures did you go on?

65 Be an animal. Or a tree.

As hard as it is to create human characters, I think it's much tougher to write about non-humans. We can try all we want and we still won't know how a dog thinks, or why orangutans do what they do. What would it be like to be a different animal?

Exercise . . . .

Write something from the point of view of any living thing that is not a human. It could be something living now (pig, coelacanth, axolotl, Venus flytrap) or something that used to live (archaeopteryx, dodo). Explain the world the way it looks to your subject. For extra points, don't say what creature it is, and see if it's clear enough for friends or teachers to guess.

66 Mythology.

It's often said that myths and legends started because the first humans didn't know how anything worked, so they made up stories to explain things like how and why the sun rises and sets, or why rain happens. This sounds about right to me, but of course we'll never know for sure, because we weren't there. Maybe they knew exactly how the sun worked but just thought it would be fun to make up stories about it.

Exercise . . . .

Invent a myth to explain something that happens in nature, like "Why the Moon Hides During the Day" or "How the Rhinoceros Got that Big Freaky-Looking Horn." (You can use these ideas if you want, but why not make up your own?)

67 Mythological zoo.

People have always been fascinated by mythological creatures: unicorns, gryphons, mermaids, etc. Most of these creatures are made up of parts of different animals stuck together in someone's imagination long ago. But that was then. This is now. We need some new fake creatures.

Exercise . . . .

Imagine a trip to the Mythological Zoo, and write about all the weird animals you see. Name them, describe what they look like and how they act. How do they react to you? Do they like being in a zoo?

68 Anti-definitions.

The trick of an anti-definition is to describe something in five sentences in the strangest or most unusual way possible, and then see if anyone can guess what it is. For example, if I say, "A ball that walks itself. Wire-spitter. Eight-toed foot. Fly night-mare. Decorator of the High Corner," can you guess what I am talking about? (The answer is below.)

Exercise . . . .

Do a list of anti-definitions, and get your friends to do the same. Read your definitions to each other, and see how many of them you can guess.

(Answer: A spider.)

69 Sound off.

My favorite part of the newspaper is the Op-Ed section. ("Op" comes from "Opinion," and "Ed" stands for "Editorial.") This is where the best writing in the paper usually is, because this is where writers get to express themselves instead of simply reporting the facts.

Exercise . . . .

Make a list of the ten biggest problems in the world, according to you. Now choose one of them and write an editorial about it. One easy way to write an editorial is to follow these steps:

❶ State the problem.
❷ Say what is being done to fix the problem.
❸ Say why this is or isn't the best way to fix it.
❹ Say what you would do differently.

You need to find out what is being done about the problem, so do your research!

70 Save the world.

I have spent a lot of money in my life on comic books. My friends and I would just sit and read them over and over, memorizing details and lines and supervillains and everyone's powers and weak points. It was a little nerdy — okay, it was very nerdy — but it helped me as a writer, because stories were often told over quite a few issues and I had to wait a whole month to find out what was going to happen next. That's called suspense; it's fun to make the reader wait.

Exercise . . . .

If you had a superpower, what would it be? How would you use this power to help people? What would your weak point be? (Every good superhero has to have a weak point, or else she or he would always win and things would get boring.) Better create a couple of superpowered friends to help you, and then a really evil supervillain for you all to vanquish.

Extra credit

Do a story in comic book form using your new superheroes and supervillians.

71 Day time.

Certain days are more important than others: holidays, birthdays, special times of the year. These times are different for everyone, and that includes you.

Exercise . . . .

Tell about the five days you look forward to most every year. Why these five days? How do they make you feel? What do you do on each of these days? Does anyone else look forward to these days? Birthdays don't count, because just about everybody looks forward to his or her birthday.

72 Adults are people, too.

As much as I hate to admit it, I have become an adult. I have a car and a house and a wife and kids and everything. But I still love talking to kids more than adults. Still, there are some adults out there who aren't so bad, who have lived a long time and have information you could use for your own personal benefit. So why not get some of that information?

Exercise . . . .

Interview five adults you know, like, and respect. (Yes, parents and other relatives count as adults, but try to find some others, too.) Ask them the following questions:

❶ What are your favorite books?
❷ Who are your favorite writers?
❸ What is the most interesting thing in the world?
❹ Who is someone you admire?

(It's okay to make up some interview questions of your own, also.)

73 What's up with hue?

My favorite color is black. Midnight sky in the Wyoming woods; gorilla fur; my car; the uniforms of my beloved Portland Trail Blazers; the color I always thought my hair and eyes were, even though they're actually brown; ink on white paper; my favorite coat and shoes; and the Goofy sweatshirt I'm wearing as I write this.

Exercise . . . .

Tell me about your favorite color. What is it? What things in the world are that color? What are all the other names for that color? Why do you think you like it so much? What does that color make most people think of? What does it make you think of?

74 A few negative thoughts won't kill you.

No matter what anyone says, it is not wrong to look at your school's faults. Personally, I like to be positive, but if you never examine your life, you can't improve it, and that goes for school too.

Exercise . . . .

Pick the one thing that bugs you more than any other about your school, and write an essay about why and how it should be changed. Don't just complain; you have to first figure out why that rule or custom exists, and see it from the school's — or whoever's — point of view. Only then can you start to offer your own better solution.

75 Lessons for the Martians.

Most of our lives are spent doing things that we have already learned how to do and we don't think about anymore: talking, walking, eating, counting, the list goes on and on. We take these things for granted, but we really shouldn't, because we are writers and we are supposed to notice all the little things.

Exercise . . . .

Describe to me, your friend from Mars, how to walk. Remember: I don't know what legs are, or that they are supposed to move one by one, because I'm from Mars and I travel around on one big slimy foot with hundreds of toes. Once you help me understand walking, then maybe you could also explain tooth brushing or how to take a photograph.

76 A picture is worth a thousand words.

Don't be afraid of art. Art won't hurt you, unless it falls on your head. But just looking at art, or doing a weird writing exercise about it? No pain involved.

Exercise . . . .

Find a book containing pictures of old paintings. Some artists to look for: da Vinci, Michelangelo, Vermeer, Velasquez, Rembrandt, Caravaggio, Corelli, and Hogarth. Pick a character in one of the paintings and write about what she or he is doing and/or thinking. You can write about everyone in the painting if you want.

77 Good self-esteem.

You are awesome. You are formidable. You rock. You have great wisdom and great skill. You deserve to be famous because you are so fabulous. Even when you don't think you're any good at all, you're still much better than just about anyone in the world. You are very talented, but you are still humble, not stuck-up at all. You are The Greatest Writer in the World.

Exercise . . . .

Write the speech you will give when you win the Nobel Prize for Literature. Describe how you got to be a great writer, and thank anyone who helped you along the way. Make sure to talk about how your favorite writers influenced you, and about what lessons young writers should learn. Who would know better than you? (Make sure you practice this speech out loud — but maybe to the mirror instead of your class.)

78 Oh boy.

We're here at a really swanky party with the following people:
Lady Ridiculous-Scenario, who can't find her necklace; Lord
Farthingless, who thinks Lady R-S ripped him off three years
ago in a land deal; young Mimi Yaya — Lady R-S yelled at
Mimi's dog last night for being in Lady R-S's yard; Baron von
Bourbon, whom Lady R-S once hit over the head with an
antique tea tray; and Annabella Belladonna Calamata, who
knows that Lady R-S was the one who made up that lie about
her at the Society Ball last year.

Exercise . . . .

So who stole the necklace? Write the rest of
the story.

79 The power of suggestion.

Readers are smarter than most writers think they are. If you want people to think of winter, you don't have to write "winter," you can say "December," or "snowstorm," or "ice skating," among many other words and phrases. In Japan, these terms that suggest seasons are called kigo (KEE-go), and there are books that list literally thousands of kigo for each season.

Exercise . . . .

Make four lists, one each for Winter, Spring, Summer, and Autumn. For each season, list all the kigo you can think of. Try doing 23 of each. Any word can be a kigo as long as it makes you think of a particular season. Try to make at least five of them unusual but real, like "Sno-cones" for summer or "the first day of baseball season" for spring.

80 Beyond suggestion.

One phrase often means different things to different people. If I write "football," some people immediately think of the snap of a cool autumn night, laughing with your friends, and the thrill of the touchdown. (I played safety and halfback.) Other people might think of too much noise, too many people, and too much violence. (My wife grew up across from a college football stadium.)

Exercise . . . .

Pick ten kigo from your lists. (Doing more is always okay.) For each, write a little paragraph that explains what feeling or mood that term produces in you. For example, if you wrote "swimming pool" on your Summer list, explain how you feel when you're swimming in the pool in the summer.

81 Get the beat.

Okay, okay, I know that you know what a syllable is, everyone knows what a syllable is, you probably even know that it's pronounced SIL-uh-bull. But let's go over it one more time. A syllable is the piece of a word you can hear as a definite beat. For example, we've already seen that the word "syllable" has three syllables: sil-uh-bull. The word "word" has only one, and "antidisestablishmentarianism" has twelve by my count.

Exercise . . . .

Try to write a story of exactly 200 syllables, and let your friends count your story to make sure. Can you write a paragraph of 99 syllables? How about a sentence of 47? Make up some tests of your own.

82 Haiku: the introduction.

Haiku (hy-KOO) is a form of poetry invented in Japan hundreds of years ago. Japanese poems have never concentrated on rhyme, probably because there are only about six rhymes in the Japanese language. Instead, they have concentrated on counting syllables. Haiku depends on two things: it must have seventeen syllables and it must have a kigo term in it. (Some people say it must have three lines with five, seven, and then five syllables again, but that's not really true.) Haiku are very hard to write — so let's write some!

Exercise . . . .

Below, I have written the first two lines of a haiku, which add up to twelve syllables. You can see that I have included a kigo, which in this case is "snowball fight." All you have to do is write the last five syllables to finish the haiku. Try a few different lines, then pick the one you think fits the mood of the poem the best. Ready? Here goes:

It's a snowball fight!
All the children laughing loud —

_____

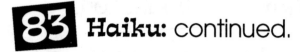

83 Haiku: continued.

The four great haiku poets of Japan were Basho, Buson, Shiki, and Issa. (Remember that in case anyone ever asks you, and look them up sometime to see how great they really were.) They kept their haiku simple and they didn't use a lot of similes or metaphors. They said what they needed to say, and then they stopped writing and let the reader's mind do the rest. (Another excellent haiku poet was named Chiyo-ni. Read her stuff — if you can find it.)

Exercise . . . .

Here is a haiku about spring, which you can tell from the kigo. However, I've only written the first five syllables, which leaves you twelve more to write. Again, try a few different approaches and maybe play around with some different ideas and moods. For example, is the sun out or is it raining? Do you like tulips or think they're stupid?

Pink and white tulips

_____

_____

84 Haiku: the big test.

All right, my friend, now you're on your own. You've followed all the steps, you've practiced your kigo, and now you're ready to write your own haiku. I'm so proud of you! Now, as I send you out on your own, I can only tell you that Basho, perhaps the greatest haiku artist of all time, once said that he would be happy if he wrote five perfect haiku in his lifetime. So don't try to be perfect just yet.

Exercise . . . .

Select a kigo from your list and write your own haiku. Write one, then look at it and see whether it works. If it does, you'll know; if it doesn't, you'll know; if you're not sure, show it to a friend and see what he or she thinks. It's okay to rewrite until you like it. Then write another haiku with the same kigo and compare the two. Which one is better? Now try a new kigo. You're on your way.

85 Haiku's lazy, funny cousin.

When I was in school, no one told me about kigo, so I wasn't really writing haiku the way I thought I was. I was instead writing a style called senryu (SEN-ree-oo). All this means is that your poem is seventeen syllables, but you don't have to suggest what season it is. Senryu are generally either funny or make some point about the world. Here's a pretty good one I wrote:

> Seventeen-pound cat lies on my chest —
> I can't move —
> Bring me an orange!

Exercise . . . .

Write a lot of senryu. Since they don't have to have a kigo, you can write them about anything, anytime, and anywhere. After a while you might find yourself thinking and talking in seventeen-syllable chunks. My brother-in-law once had to mortgage the water company and the electric company when we were playing Monopoly, and he said, "I don't need no water or power! I have candles and I have Sprite!" I of course recognized this as a great senryu.

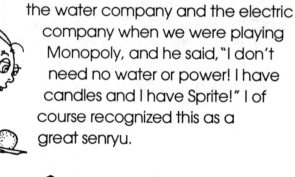

 **Competition time.**

I read in a very old book that the Japanese government used to choose its new official court poet in the following manner: the current poet would write a haiku, and all the other poets would try to "cap the verse" by writing two more lines of seven syllables each. Whoever wrote the best fourteen syllables to end the poem became the new court poet. This new poem of 31 syllables is called a tanka (TONG-kuh), and it is just as respected a form in Japan as the haiku.

Exercise . . . .

Below, you will find a haiku written by me. Add your own two seven-syllable lines to the end to cap the verse and turn it into a tanka. Then send the results to me; you will find my e-mail and regular addresses in the back of the book. Then check the Zino Press Web site (www.zinopress.com); I will choose a new winner every three months. (Make sure you tell us your age, because you can't enter this contest if you're over 18.)

> Brown leaf fell on this girl's head
> as we walked to school;
> nobody told her.
>
> _____
>
> _____

 **Linkage.**

One last vocabulary word, and it's a short one: renga (RENG-ga). This is a chain poem similar to the chain stories I was talking about in Exercise 54, but renga writing has a different structure. First, someone writes a haiku. The next person then caps the verse by writing two seven-syllable lines, and the third person (if there is one) writes a new haiku to go along with the second person's two lines. It just goes back and forth like that from there: seventeen syllables, then fourteen, then seventeen, fourteen, seventeen, etc., for as long as you and your renga-writing partners can keep it up. And when it's your turn, you don't have to read every single piece again, because each new verse should only refer to the last one, not to all the others.

Exercise . . . .

Get together as many writers as you can, but make sure it's at least two. Then pick someone to start, and go from there. Form a club and do this once a week! (This is also a great e-mail exercise.)

 **88 Last one.**

Okay, here we are at the end of the book. You've worked very hard and I'm sure you'd like a rest. Well, go right ahead, if you want, but there's something you should know. While you're taking it easy, someone else is working hard, and he or she wants to be The Greatest Writer in the World. So stop at your own risk.

This is why I write every single day. Any day when I don't write is a day when someone else might get better than me. I don't like that idea. So I keep it up, and so should you if you want to keep improving.

Look, I could only put 88 exercises in this book. There must be at least a million billion quadrillion more. Until I get to do a sequel, it's up to you to keep yourself entertained. So:

Exercise . . . .

Make up your own writing exercise. Then follow your own directions, and see how it goes. Repeat every day until you are The Greatest Writer in the World.

If you liked this book and you want to tell Matt,

or

if you want to enter the verse-capping contest,

or

if you want to send in an example
of your great writing,
Matt's e-mail address is: **zinoguy@ku.com**

If you want to see the contest winners,

or

if you want to find out more about
Matt & Brian's books,

or

if you want to learn more about what kind of
publisher would put out a book like this, and
what other books they've got, check out
the Zino Press Children's Books Web site at:
www.zinopress.com
or call (800)356-2303 for a catalogue.

If you would like to send writing pieces, fan mail,
drawings of Matt and Brian, or any other
correspondence, mail it to Matt or Brian at:

Zino Press Children's Books
P.O. Box 52
Madison, WI 53701

We're sorry, but we can't send back anything
you mail to us, so please keep copies!

If you are an educator and you want to find out if
Matt or Brian or any other Zino author can come to
your school, district, city, state, province, region, nation,
emirate, empire, solar system, galaxy, or universe, call:
(608)836-6660